Gospel Images

~ Danielle Hurley ~

Gospel Images

Daily Portraits of
God's Saving Work

God has given certain people an exceptional gift of conveying gospel truth through riveting stories. Add to that, compelling images? Then the truth hits home as nothing else. My friend Danielle Hurley is one of those gifted believers who write with gentle skill and grace. And in her new devotional book, *Gospel Images,* she augments Bible precepts and true stories through artful and stunning photography. This is a devotional book you'll want to keep next to your Bible!"
JONI EARECKSON TADA: Founder/CEO of Joni and Friends International Disability Center

The book you hold is a treasure chest of reminders of the depth of sacrificial love and grace that are yours only in God's gift of salvation through His Son, Jesus Christ. You will find your own story in each devotion as you remember your lost condition and are reminded of the earthly and eternal blessings of being adopted into God's kingdom. With each reading, you will discover immeasurable joy in your Savior and unexpected nourishment for your soul.
PAT MAULDIN: Women's Ministries, Lakeside Bible Church, Montgomery, Texas

Gospel Images is a beautiful, delightful, rich series of paragraphs and photographs that capture the beauty and truth of the gospel.
JOHN AND PATRICIA MACARTHUR: John serves as the Pastor-Teacher of Grace Community Church in Los Angeles.

In this book, Danielle Hurley makes the message of the gospel alive and practical through engaging words, appropriate images, and touching illustrations. By meditating on each day's devotion, you see with freshness that Jesus Christ is truly God and Savior. Your prayer life will be enriched, and you will want to worship God. I highly commend this book to you!
FELISTAS MBEWE: Wife of Conrad Mbewe, Kabwata Baptist Church, Lusaka, Zambia

Gospel Images
Daily Portraits of God's Saving Work
Danielle Hurley

Copyright © 2022 Danielle Hurley

ISBN 978-1-63342-112-7

Unless noted otherwise, Scripture quotations are taken from the New American Standard Bible® (NASB), Copyright © 1960, 1962, 1963, 1968, 1971, 1972, 1973, 1975, 1977, 1995 by The Lockman Foundation
Used by permission. www.Lockman.org

Cover design and typeset by www.greatwriting.org

This book is published in partnership with Sufficiency of Scripture Ministries
www.sosministries.com

Printed in Colombia

SUFFICIENCY *of* SCRIPTURE
MINISTRIES

Foreword

The apostle Paul powerfully proclaimed in Philippians 3:8–9, "I count all things to be loss in view of the surpassing value of knowing Christ Jesus my Lord." The great hymn writer, Elizabeth Prentiss, passionately wrote, "More love to Thee, O Christ, more love to Thee! Hear Thou the prayer I make on bended knee." A.W. Tozer poignantly penned, "The Bible is not an end in itself, but a means to bring men to an intimate and satisfying knowledge of God, that they may enter into Him, that they may delight in His Presence, may taste and know the inner sweetness of the very God Himself in the core and center of their hearts." J.I. Packer earnestly begs his readers, "Go, plunge yourself in the Godhead's deepest sea; be lost in his immensity; and you shall come forth as from a couch of rest, refreshed and invigorated. I know nothing which can so comfort the soul; so calm the swelling billows of sorrow and grief; so speak peace to the winds of trial, as a devout musing upon the subject of the Godhead."

What caused these great writers of the past to produce classic works? It was the reality that they lived in—and wrote from—the presence of God. As a result, what they wrote dripped with passion and feelings of divine intimacy. Their writings left you knowing with certainty that you were sitting at the feet of a godly saint whose life consisted of true devotion to Jesus Christ. What they had to say drew you into the throne room of our King and left you changed, knowing and loving Jesus Christ more. This is what makes a great, long lasting book. And this is the impact of Danielle's book, *Gospel Images*.

In a world that is filled with fanfare, tabloids, and celebrity Christianity, one is left wondering about the answer to the question, "What is this author's true character?" After searching the Internet and social media, one is merely left with an illusion of the writer's person. It is for this reason I asked my wife if I could write her foreword. I wanted the readers of this book to know that the truths powerfully penned in these pages come out of a woman submerged in the pursuit of knowing Christ. And the goal of her writing is not to sell books, but to simply help her friends experience what she longs to experience in her own relationship to her heavenly Father as she savors the grace and power of God's transforming work.

After twenty-five years of marriage to the author, I can tell you with great familiarity that the author from whom you are about to read is the sweetest, most sincere, humble, self-sacrificing, godly wife and mother I have ever known. I pray that this book will repeatedly be used to awaken, deepen, and enrapture you in the knowledge of the greatness of God's saving work, so that "you will know what is the hope of His calling, what are the riches of the glory of His inheritance in the saints, and what is the surpassing greatness of His power toward us who believe" (Ephesians 1:18–19).

Shannon Hurley
Founder and Director of Sufficiency of Scripture Ministries
www.sosministries.com

Introduction

"Preach the gospel to yourself every day." This is sound advice. But what does it look like? For the past few years, I have tried to make it practical for myself. I am a visual learner, so visualizing concepts helps me digest information. As part of my quiet time each morning, I have developed a practice of taking a mental picture of an aspect of the gospel and reenacting it in my mind. Remembering where I have come from and where God has brought me refreshes my senses of the amazing grace that has been lavished on me. And the effect? I open my eyes with inexpressible joy. Nothing brings greater joy than meditating on the love of God. Then it fuels my desire to serve my King with more fervor than ever and to mortify sin with a greater passion.

God knows how His people learn best. He knows how prone we are to forget the important and lose our proper perspective. That's why throughout Scripture, He uses illustrations to vividly portray His truth: He demonstrates His character as our Father through the realities of earthly parenting; He shows off His care for the church through the institution of marriage; and He gives countless illustrations of the gospel all throughout Scripture. I've tried to take these illustrations and place myself on center stage to deeply experience the full effect of the gospel.

So I have thought of thirty-one different illustrations of the gospel and have expressed them in short portraits in the following pages. Most of these vignettes are not situations that I have personally experienced, but that I imagine experiencing. Many of these gospel illustrations have been written through the tears of making these profound truths personal, part of my being.

Each daily reading is intended to be read as a supplement to your quiet time or in family devotions to transition you into a time of reading the Word, prayer, and worship as you experience anew the magnificent transformation wrought by the glorious gospel!

1

My Chains Are Gone

. . . you shall call His name Jesus, for He will save His people from their sins.
Matthew 1:21

Itry to shift to a more comfortable position, but the chains on my wrists and ankles don't yield enough. Most of my extremities are prickly from lack of movement. Yet I do move—I can't stop shivering, such is the cold from the icy, damp stone floor and walls. Sleep. Sleep would provide a reprieve from this misery. But the aches don't allow it . . . the aching hunger, the aching muscles, my aching heart. I close my eyes, but they don't block out the surrounding stench of human filth and spine-chilling sounds of anguish. I struggle to remember what got me into this pitiful mess. The word slams itself into my mind without mercy: *Sin.* Not that it's an excuse, but due to my heritage, I've always been enslaved to Sin. My earliest memory of my master Sin is when he forced me to do what I didn't want to do. It seemed harmless at the time, but I now see that Sin deceived me, making me a prisoner never to be released. If only I had known.

All I want is freedom. What can free me from Sin's malicious clutches? Could anything be powerful enough to be Sin's captor?

I barely nod off, hoping for some respite from consciousness. As my head begins to drop, a sudden, glaring light jolts me awake, splintering the darkness. What's going on? My eyes squint, struggling to adjust to the foreign light. A strong but gentle, scarred hand slides the key to unlock my chains and tenderly pulls me to my feet. My heavy chains crash to the floor. *Free!* I stretch my fingers and flex my feet with one arm leaning on the damp wall to steady my shaky limbs. *Finally free!* I look up with tear-blurred eyes into my Savior's loving ones. He gently directs, "Come with me." I unquestioningly grasp His outstretched hand and joyfully follow Him out of the prison gates.

> Long my imprisoned spirit lay
> fast bound in sin and nature's night;
> Thine eye diffused a quickening ray,
> I woke, the dungeon flamed with light;
> My chains fell off, my heart was free;
> I rose, went forth, and followed Thee.

("And Can it Be," a hymn by Charles Wesley)

Lord, how can it be that Your love is strong enough to break the chains of sin? I deserved to die in my sin, which was not only my prison but also my captor. I was unable to free myself from my powerful master. Why did You choose to rescue me? Because You freed me, I can now follow You. May I never look back.

Today, whenever I am tempted to complain of my discomforts or even of aching muscles, may the awareness that my chains are gone and that I have been set free from the dungeon of sin hastily fill my mind. Hallelujah, what a Savior!

2

From Enemy to Friend

For if while we were enemies we were reconciled to God
through the death of His Son. . . .
Romans 5:10

I duck behind the corner, devising my next attack. It must be brutal; it must inflict horrible pain; it must include humiliation; it must bring my enemy down and make me victor. I pace the length of my barricade. I hate him—the King who threatens my happiness by restricting my pleasures (Ephesians 2:2). My prince has set his forces against the King and I must defend my prince. After all, he gives me whatever I want.

My eyes squint in the direction of the enemy. I must preempt his attack. I try to spy his tactics. There's the King! Hatred burns in my soul. Wait—where is His weapon? It looks as though He is desperately searching for somebody. I ready my bow and steady my arrow. After I pull back to a full draw, about to release, our eyes meet. Something about His look compels me to suspend my shot. My breath catches in my throat. Unexpectedly, His eyes are full of love. In the time that I stand as if paralyzed, without lowering my gaze, my enemy starts walking toward me and is now just a few paces away. As if in a trance, I lower my bow. My enemy's hand grabs mine and motions me to follow. I want to resist! I want to fight back! But I can't. Something about Him forces me to go along, as if irresistably. We walk down the Roman road to the outskirts of the city, and my enemy's outstretched arm steers my attention to a crowd gathered in front of a cross. A gruesome semblance of a man wastes away before my eyes. It's the King's son—His only son! I turn to the King, but His head is bent, shielding His eyes, unwilling to look on the scene. His face is a mixture of horror, wrath, and grief. I look more closely at the cross and see a list. There is a long list. It is so long that the end reaches my feet. I pick up the end of the paper. It's about me—all the bad things that I have done. This is embarrassing; it is disgusting; it is unmentionable; it is . . . true. My eyes follow the paper trail to its origin where it is nailed to the top of the cross. My gaze crosses questioningly to the tearful King.

I hear words from the body on the cross, "You are dead in your trespasses. But your enemy, the King, can make you alive together with me. He forgives you all your trespasses by canceling the record of debt that stands against you with its legal demands. This He sets aside, nailing your sins to the cross, making you His friend."

I gasp to the dying Man, "You mean, You did this for me?"

But His head hangs still. I begin to shake even more than the ground underneath me. I am a murderer! I can't stay. I've got to run from here. But I can't. . . . I'm helpless.

Reading my thoughts, the King's voice interjects, "I know that you are helpless, but that's why Christ died for the ungodly."

I object, "But I am your enemy!"
He corrects me with, "Not anymore. You've been reconciled. We are now friends."

Lord, how does one turn an enemy into a friend? The answer is LOVE. Supernatural love. This love is unsolicited, undeserved, and unlimited. Greater love has no one than this, that someone lay down his life for his friends. You've made me Your friend! Lord, You should treat me as the murderous enemy that I am; instead, You welcome me as Your friend! I am a friend of God Almighty!

Lord, every time that I feel the urge to go to a friend today, may I be reminded that You are my friend, and no greater friend exists in this world.

3

Redemption from Slavery

For God so loved the world, that He gave His only begotten Son, that whoever believes in Him shall not perish, but have eternal life. For God did not send the Son into the world to judge the world, but that the world might be saved through Him
John 3:16–17

We grasp hands more tightly and look into each other's eyes on that familiar squeeze. She looks up at me with light blonde curls bouncing on her delicate shoulders. "Mommy, I want to stay with you forever. When I get married, I'll still live with you." I smile, knowing that much will change before then. We continue our morning stroll, watching boats dock at the harbor. A large ship offloads its cargo, and I watch in horror as slaves parade down the ramp in shackles. "That blue boat is my favorite. Which one is yours, mommy?" My eyes follow the slaves to the platform where some have already been auctioned off. "Mommy?" I look down to see her tugging for my attention, oblivious to this inhumane sight. I need to get her out of here—this is no place for my little girl. But one face catches my attention. It is a slave girl weeping uncontrollably on the edge of the platform. She must be barely a teenager, if that. Unintentionally, my feet move me closer to the platform. I now hear the auctioneer calling out bids for the slaves. I feel for my purse. I have the cash designated for the furniture we were about to buy. "Mommy, what are they doing to those people? Why are they hurting them?" I raise my hand and call out a bid, pointing to the young girl on the end. The burly auctioneer laughs at my incredibly low price. I raise it to as much as I have with me. He shakes his head in scorn, then looks down at my treasure and his eyes brighten. "She will be the price." She buries her face into my skirt and covers her ears. I look toward the girl who has stopped crying, watching with hopeful anticipation. This is ridiculous. I want to help, but I could never give away my precious daughter. She is priceless. I pick her up and we turn to go. I walk as fast as my legs will take me. We forgo the shopping and head straight home.

Lord, this picture is so different from what you did, because I really can't fathom offering my precious child to redeem a slave, let alone a vicious, enemy slave. I don't understand why you would sacrifice your innocent Son to release me, a sinful, antagonistic adversary. But you did. Not only that. You crushed your Son to save me. I am laid low in humility—so undeserving.

Lord, today when I see those I love the most, may I remember that You sacrificed the One You loved the most—for me. May I go about my duties in awe of Your love despite my unworthiness. I deserved punishment; You gave me new life. I love You.

4

No More Hunger

Jesus said to them, "I am the bread of life; he who comes to Me will not hunger,
and he who believes in Me will never thirst."
John 6:35

I awake from my fitful sleep. My exhaustion isn't strong enough to smother the pangs of hunger. I yield to my stomach's cries and begin the scrounge earlier than usual today. In the dim pre-dawn, I methodically rummage through the usual trash heaps, hoping for an edible treasure. My standards have lowered since this routine first began. Rotten and moldy are now viable options as I carefully place my finds into the bag on my arm. I work for several hours before my body breathlessly crumples. I open my bag and quickly and ravenously devour most of my scraps to satisfy my empty stomach, but I save a few moldy morsels for later. In just over a minute, I am finished. But the hunger pangs still cry. So, my own tears join in, and I weep. When can I ever feel satisfied? I can't exist like this anymore.

"Do you need help?" A gentle yet deep voice startles my desperate thoughts. I lift my head with blurred eyes and look into unusually kind eyes. The Man says, "Come with me." I follow Him through the garbage-lined, crowded streets a short distance. As we cross a small footbridge, we enter a beautiful landscape—a stark contrast to my world. The putrid stench is replaced by the diverse fragrances of lilacs, dianthuses, and gardenias. He leads me to a grassy seat and carefully covers me with a white blanket beside a gourmet picnic of enticing delicacies of dark, juicy berries, sweet mangos, soft cheeses, crusty bread with warm, spongy centers and tantalizing flaky pastries filled with cream. My mouth instinctively waters and I begin to reach for a pastry. "Wait!" His voice halts my first bite. "What's in your bag?" I guiltily dig and pull out the foul remains of my earlier attempts to satiate my appetite. "Give that to me." I hesitate to obey. What if I will need them later? I might die without them. Reading my thoughts, He says, "I am the bread of life; whoever comes to Me shall not hunger, and whoever believes in Me shall never thirst again." He takes my clenched fist and slowly releases my grip. He takes the crumbs and fills my hand with bright strawberries. I eat as if in a dream. I'm afraid I'll wake up tomorrow only to have to return to scavenging for scraps. But as I take another bite, I'm reassured of deep satisfaction. After tasting the greater, how could I settle for the lesser? Every day I return, and every day I am filled.

Lord, I have tasted that You are good. But, the old trash heaps still tempt me. I know that You are the only One who can satisfy, but I'm so easily allured elsewhere. If I fill myself with Your Word, the old trash heaps will lose their appeal. Lord, strengthen my faith to believe that You and You alone are the satisfaction of my soul's hunger. Help me to return to You each day that I might be satisfied with You alone.

Today, each time I open my mouth for food, may I be reminded that You are the bread of life and my supreme, constant satisfaction.

5

Adoption

. . . we might receive the adoption as sons. Because you are sons, God has sent forth the Spirit of His Son into our hearts, crying, "Abba! Father!" Therefore you are no longer a slave, but a son; and if a son, then an heir through God.
Galatians 4:5b–7

I ease the door open, hoping to avoid its creak. With one small bag on my back, I slide through the doorway, wishing to never return. After one long inhale of the crisp night air, I begin to run. I'm not sure in which direction; I only know *away*—away from this place of torture. I have spent most of my life with the distant relatives of my deceased father. They have used me only for slave labor. It was not a home; it was a workhouse filled with fear. My breathing quickens; I can't run much longer on an empty stomach. My feet pound on the damp pavement and my head pounds with fear. Where am I going? Maybe I should have stayed. What will happen to me? What if they find me? I scramble down another alley and stop to catch my breath. I need to find a place to rest. An empty box beckons my weary body. I scramble in. Within seconds, sleep overtakes me. I jolt awake to the sound of voices. "Look, Daddy! There's a girl sleeping over here!" I've been caught! Run! I look up into the early light and my eyes meet a smiling gentleman whose brows are creased with concern. "Dear, are you all right?" I sit up, rub my eyes, and see a family gathered around me. "Where did you come from, little one?" the father asks. What should I say? What if he takes me back? Something in his eyes reassures me. So, slowly at first, then gushing like a babbling brook, I disclose my life until last night's escape. The father looks into his wife's teary eyes and she nods. He takes my hands and asks, "Would you like to live with us? We want to be your parents." What? Why would they want me? I haven't done anything for them. But as I look at the other children so happily snuggling in their loving arms, I'm convinced. I nod limply, too stunned for words. Cheers erupt from the children and I am attacked as never before with hugs, squeezed hands, and bright smiles. My father's warm hand helps me to my feet, lifts me into his strong arms, and carries me home.

Abba, thank you that you are my heavenly Father! Thank you for choosing me to be Your child. You didn't choose me for my great qualities or achievements, so Your keeping me isn't based on anything I do. Thank you for Your unconditional love and care as my Father. You aren't waiting just to discipline me, but You continue to show the same compassion to me that You did when You first chose me.

Today, every time I sit at the table with my family, may I rejoice that I am now seated at Your table as Your treasured child.

6

Blind, But Now I See

On that day the deaf will hear words of a book, and out of their gloom and darkness the eyes of the blind will see.
Isaiah 29:18

I hear the sounds of morning outside my window—the birds, the noise of energetic children, and assume that sunshine is streaming into my room. But I wouldn't know whether or not the clouds have hidden the sun today. I swing my legs over the edge of my bed and feel for the slippers left near the bed last night. They are still there. I shuffle with protective hands outstretched, feeling for landmarks in my world of darkness. Darkness is all I know. I try to picture images described by those in the world of sight, but I can't really understand.

My day continues in my usual routine. Dark. My heart feels as dark as my world. What is the meaning of this effort for survival? For what am I struggling to survive? I exist in a world of searching and groping . . . .

I hear a knock on the door and slowly make my way to open the latch. An unfamiliar male voice greets me. "Today you will gain sight if you do as I say." Bewildered, I stammer, "What did you say?" He repeats his offer. I hesitate. Is this another false promise? Or, would I finally be able to see? "What do I have to do?"

"Climb to the top of Mt. Jehovah-Or, find the scroll, and bring it back to me. I'll be waiting here." I grab my walking stick and head out the door in the direction of the familiar peak, not wanting to waste any time. I follow the well-known path to the base of the mountain. The path narrows. Brambles scrape my hands as I feel with my walking stick to stay on the sloping path. I wipe the perspiration running down my forehead and hear the enticing refreshment of a brook. I don't dare veer from my path lest I lose my way. The rocky terrain steepens and twists, causing me to stumble as I step into the brush. I try to backtrack, but my foot catches on loose stones and I begin to slip. Reaching desperately for a root or branch, my hands only grasp the air and down I tumble, twisting my ankle in the fall. The choking dust cloud tells me I must have landed near the foot of the mountain. I scramble to my feet, only to find that my ankle can't bear my weight. I breathlessly collapse in defeat. Tears well up in my sightless eyes as I realize the hopelessness of my task. As I languish in the dust, I hear approaching footsteps. That same man kneels down beside me and quietly wipes away my tears. "Let me help you." He easily gathers me in his arms and commences my journey. As he trudges up the mountain, I can feel his heart rate quicken with each laborious step. Hours later, he whispers, "We've arrived." I immediately feel parchment pressed into my hands. "Open it," he urges. My fingers fumble to unroll the edge and as I spread the scroll, light enters my eyes. Blurry at first, smudges of color and shapes emerge before my eyes. I turn to look toward my Healer. My gaze is immediately drawn to the traces of blood down his arms, undoubtedly from the briars he bore in my place. My eyes shoot back up to his, "You did what I couldn't do. Thank you." He smiles at me. I look around and now focus with clarity on the millions of objects I used to only imagine. I am giddy as I race to count the leaves on the trees, follow the birds in flight, and see the color of flowers that before I could only smell and feel. I look down on the view surrounding Mt. Jehovah-Or. A whole new world is opening up to me that I never knew I was missing.

What a God!

Amazing grace! how sweet the sound,
that saved a wretch like me!
I once was lost, but now I'm found;
was blind, but now I see.

("Amazing Grace," a hymn by John Newton)

Lord, You have given me sight! It was not my own intellect that discovered
salvation, but You removed my blindness and made me see!

Lord, today, may I notice the intricacies of Your creation in a fresh way. And
each time I notice Your artistic design, may I exult in worship,
for it was You who opened my eyes to see.

7

From Rags to Riches

I pray that the eyes of your heart may be enlightened, so that you will know
what is the hope of His calling, what are the riches
of the glory of His inheritance in the saints.
Ephesians 1:18

I slip my arms into the sleeves of my shirt. I look down to button it, but the torn fabric only allows one button to fasten. I scan my home. This mud hut, consisting of only one room, has everything I need. Besides the clothes I am wearing, it has my food supply (a small sack of corn meal and dried beans), and a woven mat for my bed. My eyes survey the holes in the tin roof, through which ribbons of light stream. Yes, I have everything I need. I kneel down to pick up the jerrycan to fill at the hand-pump well. My recurrent cough flares up, forcing me to brace myself against the mud wall. A doctor visit is a luxury I can't afford. But I will survive. I step out of the doorway to the sound of a vehicle approaching. This is interesting, since vehicles only venture down my dirt path on rare occasions. Has someone died? The shiny, new, black luxury car stops in front of me. Out steps a well-dressed man. He introduces himself as the estate benefactor for my uncle who has just deceased and left me as beneficiary of his unfathomably wealthy estate. My uncle? I didn't even know him. Why would he decide to leave his riches to me? Questions swirl in my mind as the man opens the car door for me. I drop my now-useless jerrycan and ease onto the seat. The fresh scent of new leather engulfs me as I hesitantly finger the smooth seats. The interior is dust-free with closed windows and air conditioning. I've been transported into another world right on my dirt path. The car continues to roll along until we pass a very different landscape. Neatly manicured lawns replace barren dirt yards. Sprawling mansions replace ramshackle huts. I had no idea that such opulence existed. The car stops in front of the most audacious palace. Servants dressed in black and white line the front steps. The door opens for me as I am told, "Welcome home."

Lord, the inheritance You have showered me with is nowhere comparable to this feeble image of rags to riches. The riches which You have lavished upon me far exceed any earthly imagination of riches. Yours include EVERY spiritual blessing in the heavenly places in Christ, including "redemption through [Your] blood, the forgiveness of our trespasses, according to the riches of [Your] grace which [You] lavished on us" (Ephesians 1:7–8). Unthinkable riches! Your grace exceeds my most extravagant dreams.

Lord, today when I am tempted to feel discontent with my earthly resources, may I be drawn to bask in my spiritual inheritance which makes any earthly good pale in comparison.

8

From Hell to Heaven

But because of your stubbornness and unrepentant heart you are storing up wrath for yourself in the day of wrath and revelation of the righteous judgment of God. (Romans 2:5); Much more then, having now been justified by His blood we shall be saved from the wrath of God through Him.
Romans 5:9

Hell's flames are lapping at my feet, eager to devour, but not to devour into annihilation. They will devour to constant torment and terror. I have rejected God, and His wrath is about to be unleashed on me in full force. It will be constant agony, day and night, as I will gnash my teeth in the terrifying darkness, screaming for relief. I will finally understand the depth of my rejection of my Creator, and now bow before my King under the heavy hand of His fury—isolated from the One I failed to serve. I will suffer thirst but find nothing to quench it; I will feel excruciating pain but find no reprieve; I will wallow in despair but find no comfort; I will flounder in regret but find no solace; I will bawl for a conclusion but will only obtain eternity.

Just as I am headed toward this eternal damnation, I am lifted out of impending torment. Repentance barely precedes my entrance into eternity. In an instant, I find myself in an inexplicable Paradise. Sharply, I breathe in the wonder of this place—my eyes darting from one stunning thing of beauty to the next. The colors are more vivid than I've ever seen; the smells more fragrant; the sounds more beautiful. Everything I see is exactly fitted to my liking, only better. And then my gaze focuses on the greatest wonder of all—the Face. I know this Face. It is the Righteous One who brought me here. I can't take my eyes off Him. I fall down under the emotion—this overwhelming sense of adoration, affection, and intimacy. It is love—true love. I drink in His essence as I am bathed with His grace. He pulls me to my feet and, keeping my gaze fixed on His, I celebrate. I celebrate His goodness and slowly comprehend my freedom from sin, lack of shame, and removal of anger, pride, jealousy, and self-promotion. From now on, I only know goodness, kindness, humility, gentleness, peace, and joy. Perfect fulfillment replaces regret as life triumphs over death—forever.

Lord, I deserve hell. Eternal punishment is the just retribution for my sin. But Your mercy intercepted my fate. It would have been totally fair for You to have cast me into the Lake of Fire, but instead You poured out Your wrath on Your Son, Jesus Christ.

Lord, whenever I experience an injustice today, feel victimized, or even angry that I am not receiving better treatment or circumstances, may I remember that Your mercy keeps me from receiving what I really deserve . . . hell.

9

Compassionate Father

Just as a father has compassion on his children, So the Lord has compassion on
those who fear Him. For He Himself knows our frame;
He is mindful that we are but dust.
Psalm 103:13–14

I zip up my suitcase and stuff the remaining inheritance into its front pocket. I scan the room, suppressing the hint of regret as I turn my back on my family. I can't stay under this oppression of rules and guilt. I head straight for my realm of comfort—friends who share my values of freedom. There they are, waiting for me! They embrace me, then quickly reach for my inheritance. But it's okay; it will help buy my freedom. I enjoy freedom day after day, till we look into the suitcase pocket—empty. With empty smiles my friends wave goodbye. "Wait, what about our freedom?" They don't hear. They are gone. No problem; I can work for my freedom. But rejection meets every plea for work. The only available job? Caring for pigs. The wages are pitiful, and my room and board are shared with the pigs. One morning, I wake up to snouts rooting around my head. Freedom. Is this freedom? Painful memories of Daddy's loving face flash into my mind. What am I doing? Why did I reject his love? It was for freedom? This freedom? I've got to go back. But I can't, not after what I've done. But maybe I can go back as an employee, not as his child. Anything is better than this mess. I walk in the direction of the home I rejected. In the distance, the edge of the estate comes into view. Who is that running? By the uneven gate, I instantly identify Daddy. I see his familiar hair and frame marked with age, but youthful ambition sheds off at least a decade as he hurriedly approaches me. While I can still barely make out his disposition, I notice his arms stretched out, anticipating an embrace. With me? Unbelievable.

But my shame slowly dissipates as I hesitantly join in the race to reunite. Strong arms clasp around my shoulders with no sign of letting go. Daddy's body trembles with sobs. He whispers, "I am so glad you are home!" I try to pull away as I protest, "I have sinned against heaven and in your sight. I am no longer worthy to be called your son" (Luke 15:21). Daddy ignores my statement as he orders extravagant honors for me. All the pain, shame, and grief I have caused Daddy has been forgiven. He covers them with his compassion.

Lord, I have done nothing to deserve Your forgiveness. I have acted in such a way as to merit only Your displeasure. Yet You look on me with love instead of disgust.

Lord, today when I feel wronged by someone, may I remember Your response to injustice and act like You by not only forgiving them, but also lavishing them with honor. And as I interact with children today, may I be reminded of how You view me with compassion. You are mindful of my weakness, understanding that I am but dust. And as I strive to emulate You, may I see other children with Your eyes of compassion.

10

From Darkness into Light

For He rescued us from the domain of darkness, and transferred us to the
kingdom of His beloved Son.
Colossians 1:13

What naïve, uneducated thinking! I slam the door to shut out the face of my friend— my former friend. Who could be friends with such narrow-mindedness? Educated minds would never believe such ridiculous stories and follow such strict rules. She tells me of my need of a Savior, but I'm perfectly fine. I continue to pursue *my* life, *my* happiness. Unbeknown to me, I continue my virtual game of tag. I chase satisfaction, but every time I think I've found fulfillment, it vaporizes before my eyes.

My former friend won't relent. She doesn't get the hint that I don't need her religious crutch. But she perseveres and, one day, after forcefully making my point to her, the sight of her tears shocks me. I've really hurt her. I didn't know I had that in me; I'm a nice person. Out of nowhere, Light! Brilliant, dazzling, breathtaking light dawns on my understanding, and now I get it. I can now see that I'm not so nice. I have lost my temper countless times, pursued my own selfish interests, and haven't given a thought to others. She was only trying to help me. She was a true friend. Why couldn't I see it before? I do need a Savior. I rush to open her gift of the Bible and quickly find the verses she has shown me many times. Are they the same ones? Before, they made no sense, but now, these words cut my heart like a powerful sword. *Lord, I need you. Save me!*

Until now, I had no idea of the darkness of my world because I was the natural man who *couldn't* accept the things of God. But the reality of darkness was undeniable. Darkness *was* my realm until God pierced it with His glorious truth.

God has shone in my heart the light of the knowledge of His glory in the face of Jesus Christ (2 Corinthians 4:6). My former, dismal, dark heart is now filled with the light of knowledge. Everything now makes sense, has meaning, and is for God's glory, not my own fulfillment.

Lord, thank you for the light of Your Word. Thank you for opening my understanding. I am now changed to be able to see the glory of God, ". . . beholding as in a mirror the glory of the Lord, [I am] being transformed into the same image from glory to glory" (2 Corinthians 3:18). Not only can I see and understand, but I am now becoming transformed into the image of the One who has opened my eyes! Thank you for revealing Your glory to me. Thank you for letting me partake in Your glory.

Today, each time I read Your Word, may I not waste this precious opportunity to understand and know You. And each time I look at myself in a mirror, may I be reminded of how You are conforming me closer to Your image; not discouraged at how far I am from Your image, but delighted at how far You have brought me. May this fuel a greater passion to radiate Your glory every moment that I have breath.

11

From Danger to Safety

Gracious is the LORD, and righteous; Yes, our God is compassionate.
The LORD preserves the simple; I was brought low, and He saved me.
Psalm 116:5–6

My head bobs above the surface of the water, and I gasp a shallow breath just as another wave plunges me back under. I struggle for the top, but my lungs are so filled with water and my legs are so tired that it seems useless. The waves pummel me under again. My head feels cloudy and thinking grows more difficult. There is no hope. I just can't get to the surface. If only I could get one more breath! I can feel my body begin to sink. My vision is darkening and I'm blacking out. I guess this is it . . .

My tired body gives out. All of a sudden, I feel strong arms firmly grasp my own and quickly pull me up. As we enter the world of oxygen again, I heave for precious air. My sputtering turns to coughing as ingested water is expelled from my weak body. My vision hasn't returned yet, but I feel the warmth of a blanket surround my shivering arms. My dazed mind concludes that I am moving in a boat, and from the sounds of expertise and other survivors, I realize it must be a lifeboat. Strangers speak comforting words to me, and, where we disembark, the scene is reassuring. The beach is set up to receive the survivors with first aid stations, shelters, and supplies. I am ushered into a tent and assisted onto a cot. A cozy blanket is quickly tucked snuggly around me and, for the first time since the drowning, I feel secure. Comforting words whisper above me as my exhausted body finally drifts into sleep. I am safe.

Lord, You are my Savior. I was drowning without You. I tried to survive on my own, but kept getting knocked over by another wave. But You rescued me from my plight and carried me to safety.

Lord, today when fear creeps into my mind, remind me that You have already saved me from the worst possible, eternal, life-threatening danger. I can trust You to protect me from whatever You allow to come my way, whatever You filter through Your fingers of love.

12

No Condemnation

*. . . being justified as a gift by His grace, through the redemption which is
in Christ Jesus; whom God displayed publicly as a propitiation in His blood
through faith. This was to demonstrate His righteousness, because in the
forbearance of God He had passed over the sins previously committed; for the
demonstration, I say, of His righteousness at the present time, so that He would
be just and the justifier of the one who has faith in Jesus.*
Romans 3:24–26

Therefore there is now no condemnation for those who are in Christ Jesus.
Romans 8:1

My eyes remain focused on that crack in the floor, too fearful to look up as the judge seats himself again at the judge's bench. I grip the arms of my chair as I brace myself to hear his truthful words, "The verdict is guilty." I know it is true, but these are the words I have dreaded ever since I committed the horrible act. The judge's voice then interrupts my thoughts, "The verdict is not guilty." My head jerks up to face the judge. Murmurs roll around in the courtroom. His tender gaze meets my shocked one. The key unlocks my handcuffs and I am free to leave. I brush past another prisoner in handcuffs headed to the seat I had been sitting on. I overhear someone recognizing him to be the judge's son! I stop in my tracks. Proceedings begin. The crime committed is mine! I wait . . . frozen by the back door. There has been a mistake! The judge is confused; he has mixed up my file! I wait for the judge's verdict. He looks at me, then at his son, and declares, "Guilty." No! His son looks clearly innocent, and I know he took no part in my crime. He looks up at his dad with contented resignation. I want to rush to the front and clear things up, but the relief of my freedom from condemnation roots me to my place. The courtroom empties and I find that I am the last one there. I look up to see the judge. His face looks tired and drawn with emotion. "Let me explain," he says. "I know that you were guilty, but I still wanted to let you go free. But I would not have integrity if I let your crime go unpunished. So my son offered to take your punishment—out of his love for you, and his care for my name. This way, you can go free and I have still punished the crime." I barely whisper the only words I can think of, "Thank you."

Lord, this account is so unbelievable. No one would release a criminal, only to punish the innocent—especially his very own son! But this is exactly what You did—for me—so that I would be free from condemnation. If this is the kind of merciful God that You are, why do I sometimes feel as though You are waiting to strike me with Your judgment, or at least with shamed disapproval?

Lord, today when a thought of Your displeasure of me creeps into my mind, help me to evaluate my heart, confess if necessary, then rehearse Your words, "No Condemnation." And may this realization of grace not encourage me to find liberty in sin, but to have renewed vigor in fighting it.

13

Healed

*Now one of them, when he saw that he had been healed, turned back, glorifying
God with a loud voice, and he fell on his face at His feet, giving thanks to Him.*
Luke 17:15–16

I cover my face with my shawl before stepping out the front door. I check to make sure every part of me is covered, not because of the chill in the air, but because of the grotesque remains from the havoc wreaked on my body by vicious leprosy. Many extremities are now completely missing, having been destroyed by a combination of harsh elements and lack of nerves to warn of danger. God devised an ingenious nervous system, but it doesn't work for me. I pull my shawl up so that only my eyes can be seen. Then I breathe deeply before my usual call, "Unclean, unclean." I limp onto the road, trying to keep my gaze straight in front of me, avoiding the nervous mothers who quickly shoo their children indoors. One positive is the free traffic—everyone clears my path. One would think I'd get used to this humiliation, but it still stings. Every time, going out in public whips me to remember I'm not normal, but I'm actually dangerous and repulsive. I hear cries, "Jesus, Master, have mercy on us." The Healer must be near. I join in their chorus, with hopes that I would not be too repugnant to him. I rush forward as the crowd scrambles to clear for fear of contamination. I drop at the feet of the Healer. My voice quavers as I beg, "Please, heal me." His kind eyes look into my desperate ones. He replies, "Go. You are cleansed." I immediately uncover my hands. My skin is back; the fingers are whole. I begin to run after the crowds following my Healer. I have to push my way through the crowd since my unclean warning call is no longer necessary. I stumble and collapse at my Master's feet, overcome with gratitude. "Thank you!" He replies, "Stand up and go; your faith has made you well" (Luke 17:19). Immediately the grotesque deformities of my heart are replaced with a new, perfect heart. The power of sin is removed and I am healed.

> *Lord, the healing of my heart is even more dramatic than any physical healing I could undergo. But when I contemplate the dramatic transformation of being healed from leprosy, I can taste the nature of healing that came to my soul. I was decayed, repulsive, and hazardous; but You came into me by Your Spirit, making me righteous, beautiful, and useful.*

> *Lord, today every time I feel an ailment or even a headache, may I rejoice that You have healed me from a far worse condition called sin. May I continually return to my Master with profound gratitude and express my overwhelming appreciation.*

14

Loved by God

*. . . and hope does not disappoint, because the love of God has been poured
within our hearts through the Holy Spirit who was given to us.*
Romans 5:5

Love? Impossible. I can't love anyone. I've never been shown love, never felt love, never known love. I've only felt displeasure, disapproval, shame, and hate. I'm broken. Other families had models of love, but my upbringing was devoid of that piece. With the ingredient of love missing, my life will always be lacking. How can I offer what I've never received? In order to give myself the love I need, I'll just have to look on others with indifference. If I don't care, I can't be hurt. The only way to protect my already bleeding heart from further pain is to wrap around it another layer of hate. Hate? No, I don't hate anyone; I just don't love them. But I suppose that the absence of love is hate. After all, withholding love is practical hate. The layers of hate solidify with time until they harden into ice.

My icy existence continues as I walk down the dreary paths of loneliness until, one day, I stumble onto a different road. It leads me to a breathtaking scene. Water is falling from high cliffs surrounded by a carpet of green. The sun shines through the waterfall, casting dazzling prisms of light on the sheer rock that radiates brilliant luminosity. Vibrant crocuses edge the water where exotic, effervescent butterflies flutter. It is a scene of tranquility mixed with wonder. I instinctively head toward the waterfall. I hear a prayer spoken for me ". . . that He would grant you, according to the riches of His glory, to be strengthened with power through His Spirit in the inner man, so that Christ may dwell in your hearts through faith; and that you, being rooted and grounded in love, may be able to comprehend with all the saints what is the breadth and length and height and depth, and to know the love of Christ which surpasses knowledge, that you may be filled up to all the fullness of God" (Eph. 3:16–19). With that I'm whisked underneath the surging waterfall. The warm water pounds into my head God's knowledge-surpassing love. The warmth reaches my icy heart and it begins to thaw. This is uncomfortable at first, but His love sustains me as I endure the painful melting of hate into love. God's love swirls around every part of me, enveloping me. This love is inescapable, inexhaustible, and transformational.

"O the deep, deep love of Jesus!
Vast, unmeasured, boundless, free,
Rolling as a mighty ocean in its fullness over me.
Underneath me, all around me, is the current of Thy love;
Leading onward, leading homeward, to my glorious rest above.

("O the Deep, Deep Love of Jesus," a hymn by Samuel Francis)

Lord, I want to know this love even more. The more I know it,
the more I can offer it to others. Please press Your love upon my
heart so that I may be filled up to all the fullness of God. Since You
first loved me, I CAN extend Your love to others., not because I'm
naturally so loving, but because You are.

Today, every time I encounter water, may I be reminded of Your
love, and may that fuel me to draw nearer to You to enjoy the
waterfall of Your love, which pours onto me to overflow onto others.

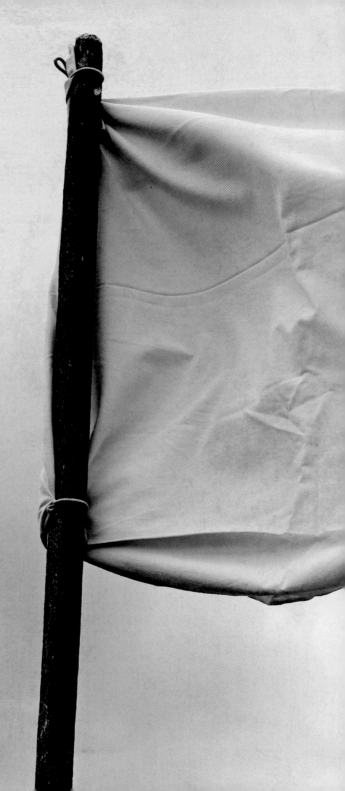

15

From Rebel to Worshiper

No eye looked with pity on you to do any of these things for you, to have compassion on you. Rather you were thrown out into the open field, for you were abhorred on the day you were born. When I passed by you and saw you squirming in your blood, I said to you while you were in your blood, "Live!" Yes, I said to you while you were in your blood, "Live!" . . . Then I bathed you with water, washed off your blood from you and anointed you with oil. . . . Thus I will establish my covenant with you, and you shall know that I am the Lord, so that you may remember and be ashamed and never open your mouth anymore because of your humiliation, when I have forgiven you for all that you have done, the Lord God declares.
Ezekiel 16:5–6; 9, 62–63

Mine. I declare it all mine—my rights, my possessions, my needs, my desires, my pleasures, my satisfaction, my esteem, my goals. And I will obtain what is mine at any cost. I am willing to tear down, degrade, slander, and abuse to self-promote. These vices actually morph into good deeds in my warped, me-centered world. I am the king of my world, with all creation existing to please me. I occasionally take a bite of religion if it serves me well, but I can take it or leave it. Others watch and secretly hope for my downfall. They wish that I would receive retribution for the wicked pain I have inflicted on so many others. Some even pray for divine judgment. The King of kings should be disgusted with such an arrogant little creature, attempting to usurp His glory and power. He should with a word throw me into eternal fury. Yet He looks on me with compassion and graciously makes me an object of His love. He cleans off the filth of my proud, murderous heart, making it pure. He turns me from a sinner to a saint, a rebel to a worshiper. Once I am clothed with His righteousness, I fall at His feet, laid low.

Lord, I was this person. My world revolved around one object—me. Yet, instead of treating me as I deserved, You looked on me with compassion and changed me. Where are the words to express my deep gratitude? I was so blind to my ridiculous rebellion that I never would have repented on my own. I was so wretched that I couldn't even see my filth. So You cleansed me yourself. Lord, forgive me for forgetting my previous condition so quickly. Forgive me for looking on others in that same condition with human, critical eyes.

Today, may I look on self-promoters with compassion, not judgment, remembering that I am just a regeneration away from that condition. And may I care enough about them to share with them Your saving message!

16

Lost Then Found

Rejoice with me,
for I have found my sheep which was lost!
Luke 15:6

The fresh mountain air is invigorating, while the high altitude leaves me breathless. The excited chatter of birds conversing about the new day fills the trees above me. My long strides carry me to a crest overlooking a serene valley below. The path appears more strenuous, so I divert from it, choosing the level grass instead. I continue this leisurely jaunt until noon when it is time to go home. I scan my surroundings, looking for the path. It is nowhere in sight. Panic briefly forces my heart to beat faster, but I breathe deeply and choose to simply turn around and retrace my steps. I continue in the direction from which I came, straining to make out the hill I had trekked. I see several more hills I hadn't noticed before. I am not sure which one is the right one. The sun creeps lower over the hills and casts long shadows over the trees. Soon, all light will be lost. I must get home. I press on, but only in vain. Night falls simultaneously with my tears. I am utterly lost. I can't go on in this darkness. Any light from the rising moon is blocked by the foliage above. I stumble over a root and brace myself on a huge trunk. I let my back slide down the trunk and sit to wait for light. Fearful hours of listening to wild nature slowly pass.

A new sound prods my attention. A low voice gradually escalates, and, as it grows nearer, I recognize the sound of my name. The voice coming straight toward me is surrounded by a glow from a brightly lit lantern. I now make out the familiar form of my father. He quickly spots me and asks if I'm all right. I heave a sigh, "I am now." He quickly pulls a blanket out of his pack and gently wraps it around my shivering shoulders. He takes my hands, pulls me to my feet, and says, "Let's go home." He guides me to the path not too far from where I was. Covered by undergrowth, I never would have found it on my own. His lantern easily casts light around my feet, warning me of roots, while illuminating the course so I know where to go. When we reach home, the gray of pre-dawn predicts an imminent sunrise. He escorts my exhausted frame to my bedroom and tenderly tucks me into my welcoming bed. When I awake several hours later, I notice a bundle on the end of my bed. I untie the string to find a map and a letter which reads, "I'm so glad I found you last night. Here is a map. Keep it close to you so that you will never lose your way again. Lovingly, Dad."

Lord, I was lost, but now I am found. I was aimless, hopelessly struggling to have direction in life, but You have given me Your Word which is a lamp to my feet and a light to my path. Your Word is also the map which shows me where You want me to go. No longer do I live in doubt or fear.

Today, each time I follow directions, may I remember that You have already given me the greatest directions right in Your Word. I will never be lost again. May my passion for Your Word be rekindled as I remember that I can't live without it!

17

Robe of Righteousness

*. . . And all our righteous deeds are like a filthy garment. (Isaiah 64:6) Blessed
are those who wash their robes, so that they may have the right to
the tree of life, and may enter by the gates into the city.
Revelation 22:14*

My fingernails are barely visible under the dark grime of dirt, sweat, and waste, but I keep digging. I frantically dig in the rubbish heap, searching for my treasure. This is a priceless treasure; it will be used as an offering for my Lord Jesus Christ. As I toss aside the moldy produce and wretched diapers, the stench begins to overtake me. I shake my head, hold my breath, and focus on the task at hand—too important to give up now and certainly worth all this effort that I repeat day after day. Oh, there it is! My offering! I carefully pull out of the bottom of the smoldering refuse several, crusty menstrual rags. I carefully fold my treasure and bring them back to my room where I kneel before my Lord in prayer. "Lord, be pleased . . . here are my offerings of righteousness. I have tried my very best to be good, to serve others, and especially be holier than everyone else. Now you may approve me." His serious voice responds, "I never knew you; depart from me, you who practice lawlessness" (Matthew 7:23).

I drop the rags in despair. But I tried my best. Isn't that good enough? The prophet's words sound clear, "But your iniquities have made a separation between you and your God, and your sins have hidden His face from you so that He does not hear" (Isa. 59:2). I collapse to the ground as the horror of these words sink in. In despair, I recognize that I have nothing to offer God. "'[Oh] God, be merciful to me, the sinner!' I tell you, this man went to his house justified" (Luke 18:13–14). Justified! Declared righteous! Through my tears, I look down at my hands. Where is the grime? I can't take my eyes off these clean, perfect hands. Where is my treasure? Out of my sight. It is back where it belongs—on the rubbish heap. (Phil. 3:8) I slowly stand up. My hands tremble as they feel to straighten my tattered, filthy work clothes. Instead of grunge, I feel only smooth, expensive sheen. "For He has clothed me with garments of salvation, He has wrapped me with a robe of righteousness" (Isa. 61:10). I lay at His feet, since no other offering is acceptable.

My Lord, I have no words. My heart is overflowing with gratitude too deep
for expression. I didn't do anything to earn this robe of righteousness. And
everything I've tried to do for you is smoldering on the rubbish heap.
Only You are mighty enough to bring me close to You.

May my day be filled with gratitude every time I look at my hands and
remember that You alone have made me clean.

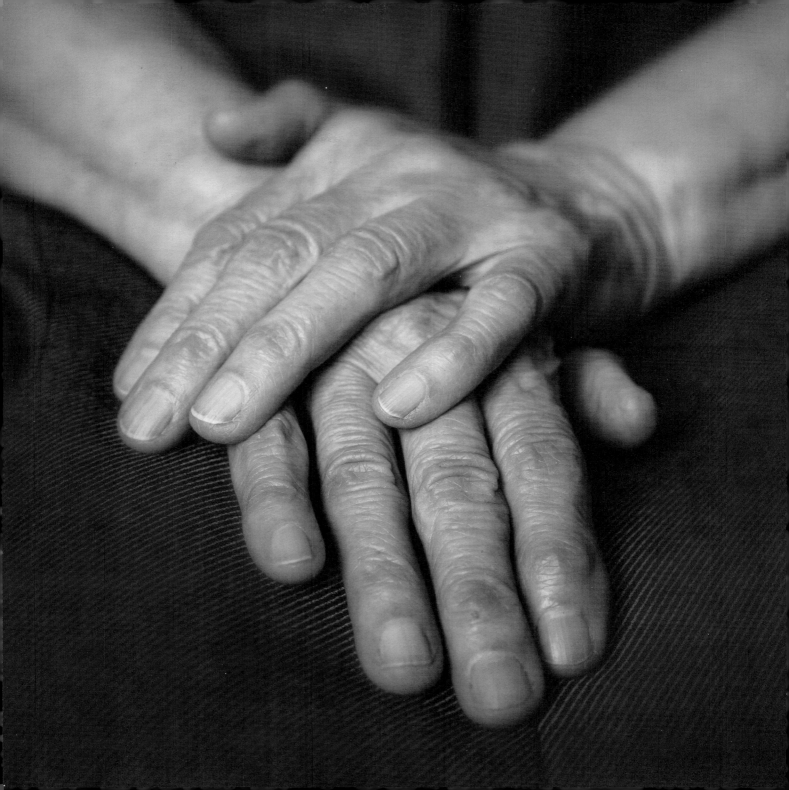

18

From Loneliness to Companionship

. . . And as the bridegroom rejoices over the bride, so your God will rejoice over you (Isaiah 62:5). Let us rejoice and be glad and give the glory to Him, for the marriage of the Lamb has come and his Bride has made herself ready.
Revelation 19:7

He was there again yesterday. It seems that everywhere I go, he shows up. It's not that he's not attractive, but I'm just not interested. I invest my affections elsewhere—in friends and entertainment. But these seemingly harmless endeavors have taken me where I never thought I'd end up . . . destitute, empty, broken, and lonely.

I have issues pressing on my heart that are screaming to dialogue with someone, but there is no one. I feel isolated, separated from all meaningful relationships. I collapse onto the park bench, head in my hands, wondering if there is anyone who cares. My teary eyes close, as the weight of despondency hurts my head.

Just then, I feel a hand on my shoulder. I turn my head to see who's there. A welcome sight greets me. He has come! This time, instead of indifference, I feel shy, self-conscious of my unkempt appearance. His kind smile doesn't show that he even notices my disheveled hair or smudged mascara. He asks me, "What's wrong?" My troubles rush back in view and my throat tightens. I can't respond. He sits beside me and I hesitantly confide the burdens of my heart to him. He listens attentively, occasionally nodding affirmation to my feelings. After hearing the details of my rebellious, wayward ventures, I expect him to look at me in disgust. But instead, he compassionately dries my tears. I apologize for the years I mistreated his kindness. He freely extends mercy and forgives me. I entrust him with my deep fears of loneliness, and he offers his friendship.

In the days and months that follow, we spend time together, become best friends, and eventually soulmates through matrimony. Loneliness has been replaced by deep companionship.

Lord, you give marriage as a picture of your love for me. Yet this human institution only reveals a glimpse of the sweet intimacy I can enjoy with you. Mary Winslow (1774–1854) reminds me that You are better than 10,000 husbands. You provide the love, protection, leadership, provision, companionship, counsel, and intimacy that we crave. Thank you for loving me first.

Lord, today when I am tempted to be discontent, either in my singleness or marriage, may I rejoice in my Heavenly Husband, knowing that in You I have more than I could want in an earthly partner. Every human will disappoint me, but You will never fail me.

"But as for me, the nearness of God is my good."
Psalm 73:28

19

Freed from Sin

Do you not know that when you present yourselves to someone as slaves for obedience, you are slaves of the one whom you obey, either of sin resulting in death, or of obedience resulting in righteousness? But thanks be to God that though you were slaves of sin, you became obedient from the heart to that form of teaching to which you were committed, and having been freed from sin, you became slaves of righteousness.
Romans 6:16–18

I did it again. I promised I'd stop. Nothing works: not the therapy, the meds, the groups, not even the centers. The habits, so deeply embedded, lead me on a chain. My mind says, "*Stop!*" But it doesn't have much influence anymore. It obediently follows my master. Day after day, I do what I don't want to do. Some days, I even agree with my master that this is good and best. But my mind knows better. Yet my mind is powerless to generate any change. I'm a prisoner to my master.

Suddenly, a strong warrior appears in shining armor and strikes down my master with one stroke. His kind eyes lock my own. The heavy metal clunks to the ground at the feet of my former master—the chain is being removed! No, the end of the chain is still on me, but unhooked from sin. Now it is attached to this new Master! I'm still a slave, but this new slavery leads me to righteousness! I am a new creation! As a slave to God, I am under His power to obey! Not only has He given me power to obey, but I am chained to Him in order to obey! The old habits are powerless. Now when my mind warns me, my body agrees and follows my new Master. Yes, I still stumble and am enticed by the old habits, but not because I'm enslaved to them . . . only because, at moments, I choose to give my members over (Rom. 6:13). Why would I ever choose the old master? I do have the power to follow my new Master! Convinced of the supremacy of my new Master, I do follow, emboldened to fight the sin which is now powerless over me!

Lord, I praise You for releasing my chains from sin, but not leaving me alone. Thank you for chaining me to Yourself! What more could I want than to be attached to my loving Shepherd! Thank you that I don't fight a hopeless battle with sin anymore. You have given me victory. Never again will I be caught in a continual pattern of sin!

Lord, today when I sin, remind me to present that member of my body to You, not to sin. It is no longer under sin's domain. So, by Your grace, I can stop choosing my old master! May my hands, feet, tongue, mind, and eyes be presented to You for worship this day.

20

From Death to Life

And you were dead in your trespasses and sins . . . . But God, being rich in mercy, because of His great love with which He loved us, even when we were dead in our transgressions, made us alive together with Christ (by grace you have been saved), and raised us up with Him, and seated us with Him in the heavenly places in Christ Jesus.
Ephesians 2:1,4–6

Dead. My life matches this description. Unable to think, respond, or act. I physically continue the mindless monotony of existence, but there is no life. When I wake up, I wish I were dead, longing for someone to cover my head with a white sheet and carry my body away. But I drag myself out of bed to join humanity's struggle for success by knocking down every threat to my happiness, with no thought for others. In order to not reveal my lack of concern toward mankind, I send a donation to the less fortunate. This boosts my ego for a moment, but doesn't satiate my craving for self. The best way to promote self is to crush the competitor, which I do well. I climb toward the top, stepping over anyone who gets in my way. With each step closer to success, my energy wanes. My shaking arms can't support my weight much longer. My trembling grip loosens until gravity wins and pulls me down through the air. I brace myself for landing on the pile of corpses. All is silent.

All of a sudden, I feel life reentering my lifeless form. I gasp to readjust to the oxygen now rushing through my veins into my pulsing heart. I open my eyes to look into the face of the Life-giver. He takes my hand and raises me. He makes me alive! Now my view of success has nothing to do with power, possessions, or self. Success is all about glorifying my Life-giver, which He even strengthens me to do. Passion replaces lethargy. Creativity crowds out listlessness. Concern for people wipes out apathy. Worship tramples love of self. This is really Living!

*Lord, thank you for not only making me alive, but raising me up with Your
Son and seating me with Him in the heavenly places! I know that
I was too dead to raise myself. It was all You.*

*Lord, today when I pass the people that You have created, may I look on them
as I once was—lifeless corpses in desperate need of hope. Lord, please give me
Your compassion to replace my indifference. May I love them enough to give
them the gospel, that they too might be made ALIVE.*

21

Quenched Thirst

Now on the last day, the great day of the feast, Jesus stood and cried out, saying, "If anyone is thirsty, let him come to Me and drink. He who believes in Me, as the Scripture said, 'From his innermost being will flow rivers of living water'" (John 7:37–38). *Ho! Everyone who thirsts, come to the waters . . .*
Isaiah 55:1

I trudge along, the fiery sand scorching my feet above my sandals. It is only morning, but the sun already burns my skin. My clothes are nearly soaked with sweat. My laborious steps sap my energy more than walking on grass, but there is no other path through this blazing desert. Hours drag on and, as I scan the barren horizon, no progress seems to be made. Salty beads roll down to sting my eyes. Dehydration mixed with fatigue blurs my vision. I miss my step and tumble, falling into the harsh sand. All I can think of is water. I slip into unconsciousness. I wake up to water entering my parched lips. I look around to take in the palm trees, green grass, and spring-fed pool. I have been rescued and delivered to an oasis! My focus immediately returns to the water offered by a caring soul. I can't drink fast enough to quench my thirst. When I've regained my strength, he helps me over to the pool, where I wade in chest deep, allowing the water to cascade all around me. I place my head directly under the downpour. The water soothes burned skin, cleansing layers of soil that slough off, revealing delicate blisters. I push back and float on my back, allowing life-giving water to penetrate every part of me. The source is so plentiful that there is no doubt of it ever running dry. The powerful surges relentlessly flood me. I think I'll stay here forever.

Lord, while I may never experience this degree of thirst, spiritually speaking, it was a reality for me. Without You, I suffered from intense thirst, unable to function in my debilitated state. But You offered, "Whoever drinks of the water I will give him shall never thirst; but the water that I will give him will become in him a well of water springing up to eternal life" (John 4:14). You are now my life-giving source, so that I truly never have to thirst again. With You, as the spring which feeds my soul, I will never again be dry, parched, or lacking. You are more than enough to give life and sustain it. All other pleasures are inferior attempts to satisfy.

Lord, today each time I bring a glass of water to my lips, may I be reminded that I already have the life-giving, life-sustaining water in You. May I remember to cling to You even more tightly, rejecting lesser offers of satisfaction.

22

God's Bridge

He made Him who knew no sin to be sin on our behalf, so that
we might become the righteousness of God in Him.
2 Corinthians 5:21

A chasm separates me from the Holy One. I attempt to build a bridge of good deeds to cross it. I think I'm making progress, until I scan the vast distance left to finish. It would take several lifetimes of perfection, and still I wouldn't be nearly close enough to reach the Holy One. I finally relent and stare in despair at the impassible rift between me and the Righteous One. I look up into the face of the Holy One and my perspective changes. Those deeds which looked pretty good before now look hideously stained with selfish motives and smeared with pride. I was seeking my glory, stealing the glory that rightfully belonged to the Righteous One. Overshadowing my tiny bridge, I can now see my lying tongue, my arrogant mind, my lustful eyes, my unkind hands, my slandering lips, my selfish feet, my unforgiving, self-protecting, angry, immoral, greedy, lazy, hateful, proud, filthy, vile, idolatrous heart. I feel nothing less than utter devastation.

Then I watch as God's own hand dares to touch my sin of pride, remove it, and lovingly place it onto His Son on the cross. He reaches down and lifts my sin of lust and carefully settles it onto His Son's back. God meticulously repeats this procedure with each filthy sin until every single one is placed on the Innocent One. It is a horrific sight. The Perfect One is laden with the heaping mass of my filth. His body sags under the weight of my hideous sin. Yet He looks into my eyes with a look that says, "I willingly accept your sin to make you righteous." At that moment, His loving Father unleashes justice. He opens the floodgates of His wrath to burst upon the target of His Beloved Son. He continues to pour the vengeance of the ages onto the Perfect One until every last drop of wrath has been absorbed by the Suffering Servant. It is finished. To my amazement, God's bridge appears. In stark contrast to my own, His is sturdy, stable . . . perfect. And He beckons me to cross.

Lord, the undeserved wrath You endured for my sake is unfathomable.
"But He was pierced through for our transgressions, He was crushed for
our iniquities; the chastening for our well-being fell upon Him, and by His
scourging we are healed" (Isaiah 53:5). It makes no sense that You would take
my punishment. I am so sorry that my sin caused You to be crushed by Your
Father. All I can say is, "Thank you." I am grateful beyond words, but I fear
that my gratitude may fade with the distractions of this world. May I never
feel entitled to any treatment greater than the wrath I deserve.

Lord, please remind me of the magnitude of Your grace each time I feel
disappointed that I don't get what I desire. May I remember, "This is
disappointing, but thank you, Lord, for not giving me what I deserve."

23

I Stand in Grace

Through whom also we have obtained our introduction by faith into this grace in which we stand; and we exult in hope of the glory of God. For if by the transgression of the one, death reigned through the one, much more those who receive the abundance of grace and of the gift of righteousness will reign in life through the One, Jesus Christ.
Romans 5:2; 17

The words come out before I realize they have been spoken. That unloving poison wielded by my most dangerous weapon that carelessly flaps out of my mouth. Of course, they are gone, and it's too late to call those words back. The guilt mounts. The regrets form that all-too familiar lump in my throat. Will I ever learn? Then I find the usual hole of self-pity that I routinely dig when I catch a realistic glimpse of my sin. With each shovelful of freshly discovered sin I unearth, my heart sinks lower into the pit. *I can't believe I am capable of doing such a terrible thing! I'm not being sanctified, but desanctified! I guess I'm not saved. How could anyone love or respect me after what I've done?* Then it comes—one drop at first. Then another. The drops of grace turn into a shower. They force me to take my eyes off my hole. With arms outstretched, I stand in position to receive the grace. For this is really where I always stand, but I can't see reality when I'm digging my hole. Now that I remember my position, I lift my head to experience the abundance. Grace upon grace steadily rains as I fix my gaze on the Giver. He loves to watch me depend on His gifts. I cry a heartfelt "*Thank you!*"

Lord, I am sorry for focusing on myself instead of Your grace. How could I think that my sin is more worthy of worship than your grace? Oh, Your grace incomparably superabounds over my sin! I can never out-sin your grace! Forgive me for being shocked at the magnitude of my sin. That only reveals how blind I really am. But it is Your kindness that shows me one glimpse at a time, so that You can gradually cut away that cancer out of my heart.

Lord, today when I am tempted to dig a hole when I feel horror at my sin, may I remember my position of grace and quickly lift my grateful eyes to the Giver of grace in worship!

24

From Earthly to Eternal

Therefore if you have been raised up with Christ, keep seeking the things above, where Christ is, seated at the right hand of God. Set your mind on things above, not on the things that are on earth. For you have died and your life is hidden with Christ in God. When Christ, who is our life, is revealed, then you also will be revealed with him in glory.
Colossians 3:1–4

The calendar bulges with busyness, activities, recreation . . . . What's the next amusement, pleasure, diversion to beguile me from reality? Life brings heartache, worry, and fear. So I smother my discomfort with entertainment. I vicariously live the intrigue of imaginative characters in movies, shows, and books. I attempt to recreate their enchantment by pursuing my own world of pleasure. So I buy comforts and indulge in the next fun pastime. I fill encroaching voids with social media updates, never giving the silence an opportunity to reveal the emptiness—always looking ahead, always pursuing more. It is never enough. Little do I realize that my pursuits keep my feet trudging through muck which bogs my pace and forces my downcast eyes to see only the filth and mess of my slog which deceitfully appears as enjoyable.

But truth penetrates understanding. I feel my legs and arms lifted out of the mire—higher and higher, until I'm no longer in this world. Now raised with Christ, my old self is dead; marred reality is replaced with undeniable verity. From this lofty vantage point, my survey is clear. Those previous, pleasurable pursuits are now seen for what they really are—pitiful endeavors for gratification while true fulfillment lies out of reach. The trivial efforts are exposed for what they actually are: laborious plodding through the grime, not honorable quests for fulfillment, as I formerly misperceived them to be. Up here, the air is clear; the view is vast; the outlook promising. I see now that the quest isn't for my temporary, earthly happiness, but for permanent, eternal joy. I gladly set my mind on things above to exchange the earthly trash for the treasure of Christ.

Lord, You brought me out of the mire and have put me on the path to live with You—forever. That is true life. This one is but a vapor. What mercy to remove my lesser pursuits and replace them with enjoyment of You. Lord, I want to be prepared to meet You face to face.

Today, as I encounter the inevitable distractions which tempt my mind to dwell on the earthly instead of eternal, please lift my eyes to worship. May each potential worship robber actually remind me to set my eyes on things above and on the One whose mercy has given me hope of life with You.

25

Faith Produces Righteousness

For all have sinned and fall short of the glory of God, being justified as a gift by his grace through the redemption which is in Christ Jesus; whom God displayed publicly as a propitiation in his blood through faith. This was to demonstrate His righteousness, because in the forbearance of God He passed over the sins previously committed; for the demonstration, I say, of His righteousness at the present time, so that He would be just and the justifier of the one who has faith in Jesus.
Romans 3:23–26

The gavel crashes to the Judge's desk for the thousandth time: "Not Guilty!" Spectators gasp in bewilderment as yet another guilty convict is released. He leaves to follow the other murderers, thieves, liars, insubordinates, gossips, complainers, and worriers who are set free from eternal condemnation. Shouts ring out from the gallery: "Injustice!" "This is wrong!" and "How could you do this?" The Judge simply remains silent until the next convict approaches the stand. He hears the name of the convict and looks in His Book of Life. The name is missing, and He pronounces, "Guilty!" The convict tries to protest, but is led away to eternal condemnation. Another convict approaches the stand. The Judge easily finds his name in the Lamb's Book of Life next to all who were given the gift of faith—true, saving faith, which was "credited to him as righteousness" (Rom. 4:22). The crowd again rises in an uproar, knowing the hideous past of this man. Then all eyes converge to an event being played out in the backdrop of the Judge. A cross is erected behind Him on which hangs the Judge's very own Son. The unmentionable atrocities committed by the released convicts swirl together until they form a raging storm cloud of dark destruction. The cloud hovers, then rests onto the sagging, corpselike body of the Savior. At the touch of such wickedness, He cries out as never before, feeling sin for the very first time. The pain of the sin and isolation from His Father far outweigh the physical torture of the cross. Finally, after absorbing the full torment of sin, He cries, "It is finished!" The Judge accepts the next convict and when his name is found in the book, He gestures to the now empty cross in the background. The spectators don't protest this time, but nod in agreement. Justice has been met.

Lord, You save the same way You always have, but before Christ died, You put their punishment "on hold." But it has always been the same method— saving faith produces Your righteousness. And only by Your righteousness was my name written in the Lamb's Book of Life. Thank you that my salvation is not up to me. And thank you for choosing me.

Lord, today when I feel guilt for my sin, please help me to remember that You have declared me, "Not guilty!" You've set me free from the sin for which I've been forgiven. And even though I will inevitably sin again, even all my future sin is forgiven! Thank you for the cross!

26

Not by Works

For as many as are of the works of the Law are under a curse; for it is written, "Cursed is everyone who does not abide by all things written in the Book of the Law, to perform them." Now that no one is justified by the Law before God is evident; for, "The righteous man shall live by faith."
Galatians 3:10–11

The list lies on the table, but that is the only thing there. That to-do list stirs up my heart into a frenzy, even a panic. There is so much to do, such a load to get done. It includes the normal essentials for running a home but has another long trail including ministry items . . . service projects, meetings to attend, notes to write, people to call, meals to provide, lessons to teach, crafts to prepare—and that is only for today! I know it seems like too much, but it is only a fraction of what I should be doing; I know that it still isn't enough to please the Lord. I rush out of my bedroom and begin to bark the orders that will enlist the troops into action. "Room checks in two minutes. Breakfast in three. Who left the wet washcloth on the bathroom floor? No, you may not invite your friend over; your siblings are your friends, and I am too, of course," I rage. "Change your hair—not so spiky. Whose music is playing so loudly? Begin your second set of chores. I have a lot to do!" I whirl around and mow down the fragile one, whose wails awaken me to the reality of my inadequacies. I try so hard to serve God and my family but, obviously, I can't. Why can't I attain perfection? Instead, I've created a world of pressure, duty, reliance on the law, and void of Christ. I simply wanted to do enough. The pressure of the standard presses me down to my knees. I have always relied on myself, been competent, and able to model godly living (in the public eye).

But, today, I see that my attempts are failing. It's not working. How is my screaming at my children any less sinful than the lies they use to cover up the dread of their mistakes being found out? I am completely unable to do enough or make myself good. If I want to be righteous, it must be by faith—not by list! I gather my flock from their duties and confess to them, "I have been wrong, so wrong. I've been leading you to believe we can all be good enough. But we can't. Lord, I beg you to give me your gift of faith. I can't keep your standard on my own."

Lord, thank you for removing the curse of my inability to do enough. The heavy hand of the law has been lifted. Lord, thank you that You provide a righteousness outside of myself. That way, You receive the glory from any good I might accomplish through You. Any good works I can perform are a result of Your work in me. Help me to serve out of my passion for You, not out of duty. (See Titus 2:14.)

Today, with each task I perform, may I be reminded that it is not to earn any praise from You or from man. May my motivation be my love for You. Help me to remember that I am never more like You than when I serve You with a joyful heart!

121

27

Unpayable Debt

Remember that you were at that time separate from Christ, excluded from the commonwealth of Israel, and strangers to the covenants of promise, having no hope and without God in the world. But now in Christ Jesus you who formerly were far off have been brought near by the blood of Christ.
Ephesians 2:12–13

Debt. The word itself brings a chill to my spine when I consider the gravity of mine. For the thousandth time, I calculate the wages necessary to pay it back. If I were to work many lifetimes, I still could not earn enough to pay off this outrageous debt. And the thought of failure to pay unleashes through my mind nightmarish flashes of debtors' prison. I quicken my pace along the bustling streets, searching more earnestly for work. Rejection has met every plea. It's not that I'm unwilling to put in a hard day's labor, but work is hard to find, especially work that could significantly whittle down my debt. At the end of another fruitless day, I trudge along the endless streets of this harsh city. Debtors' prison inevitably looms in my too-near future. I deserve it. I just can't pay my debt. I set off in the direction of the foreboding building and prepare to turn myself in. I walk up the entrance steps as my benefactor opens the front door. At the sight of him, I immediately cower in shame. I begin to confess my failures, admitting my inability to ever repay. Before I can deliver myself into his custody, he declares, "Paid in full." "What? I have just explained that I can't possibly pay it back." He nods in understanding, then continues, "That's why I have paid it in full. Go. You're free."

I turn from the dark, prison walls, too overwhelmed for words, and hesitantly step away. My debt has been erased! Immediately, I turn back and am drawn to my Redeemer. "I'm Yours. I gladly offer my services and my life to You."

Lord, when you died, You bore my sin. And it was priceless. I could never have paid enough or done enough to rid myself of my burden of sin. But You could. And You did. My guilt doesn't incapacitate me anymore. Sure, I still feel it. But rather than contemplating my guilt, now I can lift my eyes toward the cross—the place where my guilt is finished.

Each time I am tempted to focus on my shame, remind me to lift my eyes to see Your glorious Son. Oh Lord, thank you for being the lifter of my head so I can see Your work on the cross! You are worthy! Thank you for paying my debt!

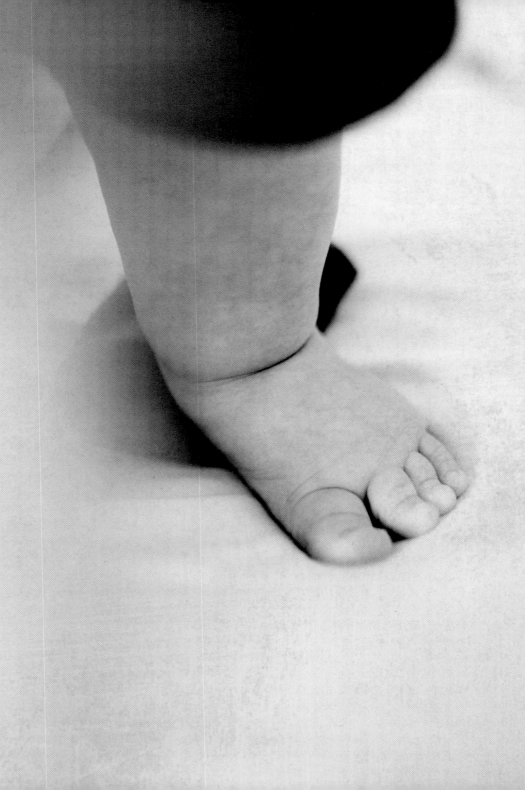

28

Self-sufficient to Dependent

For while we were still helpless, at the right time Christ died for the ungodly.
Romans 5:6

"It's okay. I've got it. Don't worry, I can handle it." This is my mantra as I navigate the obstacles of life. I love my independence. I live and fight for freedoms: freedom from authority and anything that would dare to threaten my rights for happiness. I am generally upbeat and only unsheathe my "rights sword" when I need to protect myself. I am capable of taking care of myself, thank you very much. I know what I need and how to get it. We will all be fine as long as you don't stand in my way.

But Someone does stand in my way. The King of the universe makes His name known, which humbles me to the ground. He strips me of my armor of independence, self-sufficiency, resources, and abilities. I become needy. All of the supports, which I have always found my confidence in, have been detached. I tremble, kneeling in the dust, looking wildly for a solution. Just as I attempt one last thrust into the air with my sword of "rights," He gently disarms me. Empty-handed, I finally realize the reality of my helplessness. It's uncomfortable. It feels too vulnerable. But my King begins to instruct my thinking. Similar to physical therapy, He repetitively reinforces dependence on Him. He begins by taking both of my hands and gently lifting me to my feet. Then, he teaches me as with baby steps how to walk—this time, only holding onto His strong arm for support. I begin to learn to trust His faithfulness. But when my fears overtake my young faith, I let go of Him and reach out for my former supports. Those previous sources of reliance inevitably fail to catch me. Each time I fall, He grabs hold of my hands to rescue me. He continues to prove trustworthy. He strengthens my baby steps until eventually I am willing to dive from great heights into His arms. Many times, it doesn't look like He will catch me. Many times, I can't feel His presence or I find myself in a situation I would not have chosen, but He never fails to be faithful. I am learning to lean on my King in dependence.

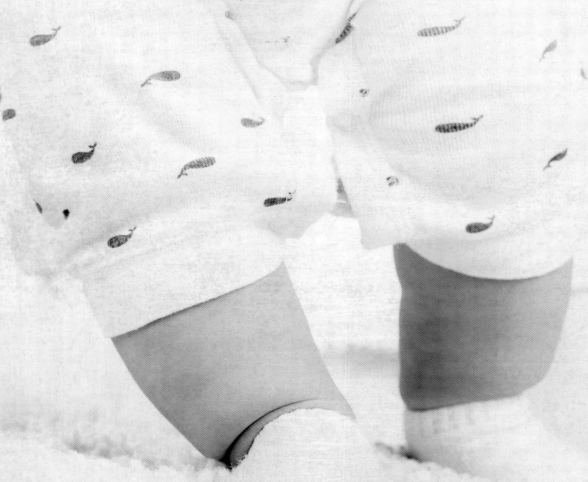

Lord, thank you for being all-powerful and all-sufficient. Thank you for showing me that I need You. I want to see my need for You even more. Even though You have shown me my helplessness, I forget, and regress to my self-sufficient ways. My problem is that I don't see how fragile and vulnerable to sin I am without You. I don't understand that I desperately need to depend on Your Spirit. I don't truly believe that I can't survive a single second without You as my helper, guide, teacher, and counselor.

So, today, please grant me a heightened awareness of my utter need of You, that I would rely on You completely, for You are faithful.

29

Inaccessible to Intimate Access

You shall hang up the veil under the clasps, and shall bring in the ark of the testimony there within the veil; and the veil shall serve for you as a partition between the Holy Place and the holy of holies. You shall put the mercy seat on the ark of the testimony in the holy of holies (Exodus 26:33–34). There I will meet with you; and from above the mercy seat, from between the two cherubim which are upon the ark of the testimony, I will speak to you about all that I will give you in commandment for the sons of Israel.
Exodus 25:22

And behold, the veil of the temple was torn in two from top to bottom; and the earth shook and the rocks were split.
Matthew 27:51

I seek an intimate relationship with God Most High. I long to be near His presence, so I enter through the eastern gate. I step into a vast courtyard filled with other worship-seekers. Reverence permeates as hushed pleas and praises swirl. I inhale deeply to imbibe the awe of this place, but as I do, a stench fills my nostrils. Burning life and flesh overwhelm me. I stand near the altar where the punishment for my filth is incinerated. Priests serve tirelessly with blood-soaked hands to atone for my sin and restore the peace with my Creator that I have destroyed. Behind the inner sanctuary lies the most precious place on earth, the sacred cube (1 Kings 6:20). Inside lies the mercy seat, lined with gold and guarded by cherubim. Beneath the seat of mercy rests an impossible law. Broken countless times each second, the law waits impotently in the ark. But just above the law, blood is sprinkled onto the mercy seat, staining the brilliant gold so that the lawbreakers' sin can be atoned. After offering monotonous sacrifices over days, years, centuries, and millennia, God's people strain for redemption—one that will atone for lawbreaking once and for all.

Then, when least expected, a new High Priest is incarnated. However, this High Priest is not anointed by human choice, but by God Himself. Despite His righteous life, the blood-stained priests resent Him, putting His holiness on trial. Priests plot and scandal ensues. Instead of focusing on their duty of offering atonement, the priests pronounce blasphemy and treason to prevent the very redemption they have spent their lives foreshadowing. Prepared for resistance, the elite leaders are surprised as the High Priest willingly offers Himself as a Lamb upon the altar. Blood drenches the sacrifice, satisfying God as never before. Words drift from the wooden, cross-shaped altar, "Father, forgive them, for they don't know what they are doing" (Luke 23:34). The hand of God Almighty tears the massive fabric that separates man from God, exposing the Most Holy Place. This sacred cube where the presence of God came to dwell is now accessible. Access to the Holy One is now immediate and intimate. I now boldly enter the Most Holy Place . . . and worship.

Lord, what can I say? For millennia, God-fearers labored to gain access to Your mercy. The law and the blood were daily infused into the consciences of anxious believers. But You tore the curtain in two. No more hoping for redemption from sin's oppression. Redemption has come; I now have this once-coveted relationship with God Most High. The presence of God Most High no longer resides in a physical temple, but in the temple of our hearts! And it gets better; I have hope of a perfect future relationship when the New Jerusalem (Revelation 21:16) descends in the same proportions as the Most Holy Place, and You Yourself will be the Temple! I will dwell without the stain of sin and enjoy unimaginable intimacy with You.

Today, when I notice the dimensions of any room that resembles a cube, may I rejoice that I will enjoy You forever in an enormous cube which will house Your glory. May I live for that world, not this one.

30

Cast My Crown

For we must all appear before the judgment seat of Christ, so that each one may
be recompensed for his deeds in the body, according to
what he has done, whether good or bad.
2 Corinthians 5:10

My name is called. I enter the throne room and my gaze fixes on my radiant Lord. The flashes of lightning blaze dangerously close to me. Peals of thunder roll underfoot. Beyond the brilliance, the throne, lofty and exalted comes into view. Right in front of the throne sits the bema seat, the place where God judges believers. I have always known this day would come, when I would meet my Maker to give an account for all the things that I have done. I reverently approach the judgment seat, feeling especially small in the grandiose hall. Although I know that His righteousness has freed me from all condemnation, I still hesitate as I wonder if I have spent my life on eternal value. I linger before the Holy Judge, then carefully kneel before the seat, and feelings of my unworthiness flash through my mind. Fear grips me as I quickly recall my proud and selfish motives, even for my good deeds. As my heart is exposed by God's holy presence, I wonder if there is anything I have done of value during my vaporous life. At that moment, Jesus Christ breaks into my doubts and announces, "My grace is sufficient for you. My blood has made you righteous and brought you near to God. Well done, good and faithful servant. Enter into the joy of your Master" (Matthew 25:21). I quickly exhale the breath I have been holding in suspense and open my tightly squeezed eyes to focus on the throne. I now see the Lamb who was slain, seated on the grandeur throne. My gaze is transfixed as I behold this innocent, perfect Lamb with deep, blood-red scars—the price of my redemption. Christ bends down and places a crown of righteousness onto my head. I can't look up. This grace is too overwhelming! I don't deserve this! What can I do to say thank you? I fumble for an appropriate response. Then I carefully finger the crown and with trembling hands, gingerly remove it from my head. Tears of joy mixed with gratitude stream down my face as I cast the precious crown where it belongs . . . at the foot of the throne, at the feet of Jesus.

Worship. The only suitable response to Your gift of grace. Lord, I clearly don't deserve Your imputed righteousness. For reasons I don't understand, You chose me to inherit Your salvation. And one day, I will possess it in its fullness! (Ephesians 1:14) And I will have the privilege of casting my crown of righteousness at Your feet. Until then, Jesus, I want my short life to radiate with praise to You. I want every hint of self-promotion to dissolve as I am enamored by You.

Lord, help my self-protection to be swallowed up by joyful self-denial. Turn my self-gratification to cheerful sacrifice for the glory of Your name! May I anticipate with childlike giddiness each opportunity to worship by constantly casting my crowns at Your feet throughout today.

31

From Glory to Poverty

. . . I saw the Lord sitting on a throne, lofty and exalted,
with the train of His robe filling the temple.
Isaiah 6:1

. . . but emptied Himself, by taking the form of a bond-servant,
and being made in the likeness of men.
Philippians 2:7

"Holy, Holy, Holy, is the Lord of hosts, the whole earth is full of His glory," cry out the Seraphim one to another. Incessant praise reverberates around the throne which is so filled with glory that the haze of smoke covers the vast, radiant throne room. The focus of Heaven is all directed to this common Person—The Lord Jesus Christ. Then before another exaltation can be uttered, the adored King steps off His throne, telling us, "You know how much I love mankind. You remember how I walked with them while they were sinless. And on the day when they lost their innocence, My Father promised that I would crush the Serpent's head. But first, he must bruise My heel. It is time for Me to buy back My priceless treasures." The Seraphim, Cherubim, and Archangels nod in agreement, without full comprehension. They immediately transfer their gaze on a young, fragile human who carries Him in her womb. They are awed by this incongruity and watch with eagerness. Nine long months pass until their King comes into view again—now visible in an unsanitary bed of straw near filthy creatures. Nothing could create a more stark contrast to His former home of glory. The angels continue to watch their King grow up in an impoverished home, while earthly kings lavish themselves with opulence. The King of kings carries out menial chores worthy only of the lowest slave. His hands get dirty; He is plagued with hunger, thirst, exhaustion, and sickness. He grows into a man who begins to minister for His Father. *Now*, the angels hope, *He will be treated like the King He is*. Their desires are shattered as their King continues to live like a servant, hastening to meet the demands of the crowds clamoring for healing. *This is wrong. These humans are not worshiping our King; they are commanding Him according to their own desires.* The angels watch their King continually clothe Himself with the apron of humility, even washing the feet of His helpers. But the most grueling scene to behold is when their Perfect One silently accepts false accusations and subjects Himself to utter humiliation, suffering, and impending death. *No!* the Guardians protest. *This can be stopped! We are ready to swoop down, carry Him away, and destroy all these enemies of our King.* But they only hear, "Father, forgive them, for they know not what they do" (Luke 23:34). *Who are these humans who would elicit such love from our Creator?*

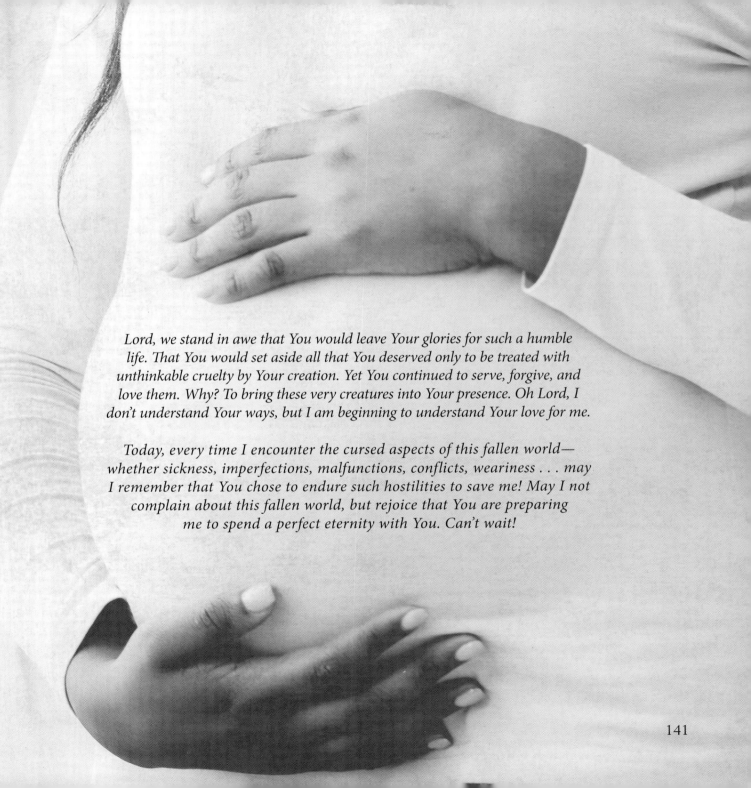

Lord, we stand in awe that You would leave Your glories for such a humble life. That You would set aside all that You deserved only to be treated with unthinkable cruelty by Your creation. Yet You continued to serve, forgive, and love them. Why? To bring these very creatures into Your presence. Oh Lord, I don't understand Your ways, but I am beginning to understand Your love for me.

Today, every time I encounter the cursed aspects of this fallen world—whether sickness, imperfections, malfunctions, conflicts, weariness . . . may I remember that You chose to endure such hostilities to save me! May I not complain about this fallen world, but rejoice that You are preparing me to spend a perfect eternity with You. Can't wait!

From the Author

Dear Friend,

Thank you for allowing me the privilege of sharing with you my own personal meditations on the gospel. My prayer is that this would not be the end of your focus on the gospel, but only some inspiration to make preaching the gospel to yourself a normal part of your routine.

Hopefully an image or two that you have just seen and read will be embedded in your memory so that the next time you are tempted to dwell on unbiblical thoughts that will lead to sin, discouragement, and distraction, your mind will be renewed with the truth that will lead you to worship Christ for all that He has done for you. It is this bolstering of our minds in the truth that strengthens the roots of our faith to be prepared for the next storm that is sure to hit. And when that storm comes, whether in the form of a soft shower or a violent hurricane, come, revisit *Gospel Images* for a refresher of the truth of your position in Christ.

Press on, my dear friend! We have been loved, adopted, healed, freed, and made righteous for a future reality! Let's keep our eyes on Jesus, the author and perfecter of faith, that we may not grow weary or fainthearted till our journey's end!

Fellow Pilgrim,

Danielle

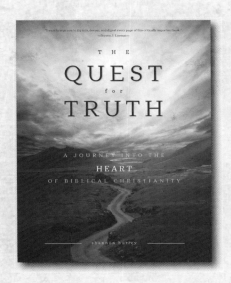

The Quest for Truth | Shannon Hurley | Large Paperback, 248 pages
ISBN 9781633421820

This is more than just a book; it is a road map. It is penned with passion, concern, and thoughtful consideration for its readers. It provides guidance through the wonderful teaching of God's Word, the Bible, in a systematic and comprehensive way. It does not assume that its readers have a lot of knowledge, and it cuts a careful course through key Old Testament and New Testament aspects of the gospel of the Lord Jesus Christ. Readers working their way through this—whether as individuals or in a group—will complete the fifteen chapters with a robust and comprehensive understanding of God-centered Christianity.

"...a helpful primer to Christian thought...."

—John MacArthur

"...I highly recommend it for personal study, small groups, or the classroom!"

—Joni Eareckson Tada

About Shepherd Press Publications

They are gospel driven.
They are heart focused.
They are life changing.

Our Invitation to You

We passionately believe that what we are publishing can be of benefit to you, your family, your friends, and your work colleagues. So we are inviting you to join our online mailing list so that we may reach out to you with news about our latest and forthcoming publications, and with special offers.

Visit:

www.shepherdpress.com/newsletter

and provide your name and email address.